A HAPPY BIRTHDAY

The Book of
BIRTHDAYS

From Connie and Selynn
May 24, 2006

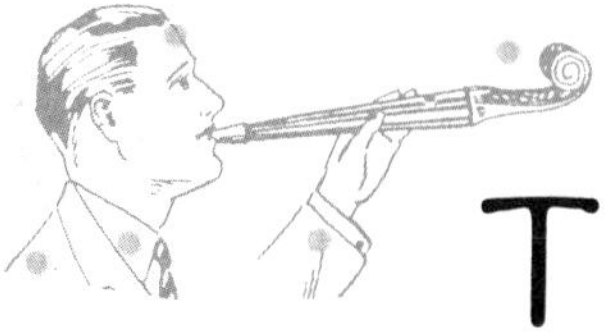

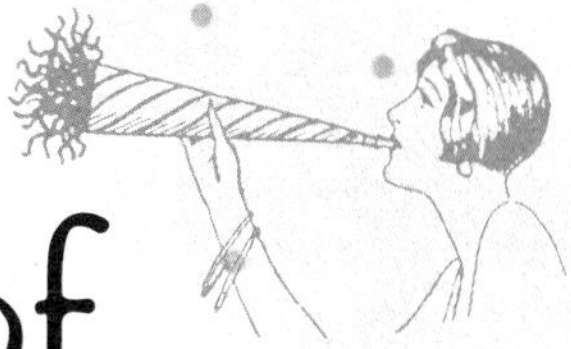

The Book of BIRTHDAYS

Edited by Lorraine A. DarConte
Designed by Diane Hobbing

Ariel Books

**Andrews McMeel
Publishing**

Kansas City

ISBN: 0-7407-2210-7
Library of Congress Catalog Card Number: 2001096951

CONTENTS

Let Them Eat Cake   123

INTRODUCTION

Everyone has a birthday—and whether you announced your arrival by howling at the top of your lungs or quietly sucking your thumb—that day, now and forever, is cause for celebration. Although birthdays may seem like frivolous occasions, they are indeed important milestones in our lives, whether it's our first birthday, sixteenth, thirtieth, or sixtieth.

Hundreds of years ago birthdays were actually thought to be dangerous because they marked a change in a person's life. This change, it was believed, could cause evil spirits to inflict harm upon the person whose birthday it was. Hence, people believed if they visited friends and relatives on their birthday, they could help protect them. That protection included the use of noisemakers to scare the evil spirits away.

Much has changed since then, and most people, children in particular, look forward to each birthday with great anticipation, hoping to receive a particular toy or perhaps a pair of very cool sneakers. For kids, birthdays are perhaps the best day of the year. Adults, on the other hand, sometimes grimace at the thought of yet another birthday, wondering how it is the years manage to fly by so quickly.

Celebrating your birthday allows you to take a break from your daily routine—to stop and reflect on the past year and perhaps make plans for the new one. It's also a great excuse to throw a party (for someone you love, including yourself) or treat yourself to something special—dinner at a favorite restaurant, that new stereo set you've been eyeing for months, or even a trip to Paris. This book is a patchwork of recipes, games, trivia, poems, passages, words of wisdom, and more to help you both celebrate and remember your very special day.

HAPPY BIRTHDAY

Monday's Child Is Fair of Face

Monday's child is fair of face,

Tuesday's child is full of grace,

Wednesday's child is full of woe,

Thursday's child has far to go,

Friday's child is loving and giving,

Saturday's child has to work for its living,

But a child that's born on the Sabbath day

Is fair and wise and good always.

—Anonymous

Happy Birthday 17

A birthday . . . a good time to begin anew: throwing away the old habits, as you would old clothes, and never putting them on again.

—Bronson Alcott

Happy Birthday 19

Today I feel happy. What a day—
no clouds in the sky!

—Charles Baudelaire

One to-day is worth two
to-morrows.

—Benjamin Franklin

Happy Birthday 23

I shall grow up, but never
grow old . . .

—Charlotte Mew

Happy Birthday 25

The Salutation of the Dawn

Listen to the Exhortation of the Dawn!

Look to this Day!

For it is Life, the very Life of Life.

In its brief course lie all the

Verities and Realities of your Existence;

The Bliss of Growth,

The Glory of Action,

The Splendor of Beauty;

For Yesterday is but a Dream,

And Tomorrow is only a Vision;

But Today well lived makes every

Yesterday a Dream of Happiness, and every

Tomorrow a Vision of Hope.

Look well therefore to this Day!
Such is the Salutation of the Dawn.

—From the Sanskrit

Happy Birthday 27

Languor is underrated. Bone-lazy idleness, hours spent staring at the sky and remembering books and birthdays and great kisses: this is a pure pleasure . . .

—Kevin Patterson

The real trouble with old age is that it lasts for such a short time.

—Sir John Mortimer

Wishing you a happy * birthday

From *A Little Princess*
by Frances Hodgson Burnett

[Sara's father] had made wonderful preparations for her birthday. Among other things, a new doll had been ordered in Paris, and her wardrobe was to be, indeed, a marvel of splendid perfection. When she had replied to the letter asking her if the doll would be an acceptable present, Sara had been very quaint.

"I am getting very old," she wrote; "you see, I shall never live to have another doll given me. This will be my last doll. There is something solemn about it. If I could write poetry, I am sure a poem about 'A Last Doll' would be very nice. But I cannot write poetry. I have tried, and it made me laugh. It did not sound like Watts or Coleridge or Shakespeare at all. No one could ever take Emily's place, but I should respect the Last Doll very much; and I am sure the school would love it. They all like dolls, though some of the big ones—the almost fifteen ones—pretend they are too grown up."

Captain Crewe had a splitting headache when he read this letter in his bungalow in India. The table before him was heaped with papers and letters which were alarming him and filling him with anxious dread, but he laughed as he had not laughed for weeks.

"Oh," he said, "she's better fun every year she lives. God grant this business may right itself and leave me free to run home and see her. What wouldn't I give to have her little arms round my neck this minute! What wouldn't I give!"

The birthday was to be celebrated by great festivities. The schoolroom was to be decorated, and there was to be a party. The boxes containing the presents were to be opened with great ceremony, and there was to be a glittering feast spread in Miss Minchin's sacred room. When the day arrived the whole house was in a whirl of excitement. How the morning passed nobody quite knew, because there seemed such preparations to be made. The schoolroom was being decked with garlands of holly; the desks had been moved away, and red covers had been put on the forms which were arrayed round the room against the wall.

When Sara went into her sitting room in the morning, she found on the table a small, dumpy package, tied up in a piece of brown paper. She knew it was a present, and she thought she could guess whom it came from. She opened it quite tenderly. It was a square pincushion, made of not quite clean red flannel, and black pins had been stuck carefully into it to form the words, "Menny hapy returns."

"Oh!" cried Sara, with a warm feeling in her heart. "What pains she has taken! I like it so, it—it makes me feel sorrowful."

But the next moment she was mystified. On the under side of the pincushion was secured a card, bearing in neat letters the name "Miss Amelia Minchin."

Sara turned it over and over.

"Miss Amelia!" she said to herself "How can it be!"

And just at that very moment she heard the door being cautiously pushed open and saw Becky peeping round it.

There was an affectionate, happy grin on her face, and she shuffled forward and stood nervously pulling at her fingers.

"Do yer like it, Miss Sara?" she said. "Do yer?"

"Like it?" cried Sara. "You darling Becky, you made it all yourself."

Becky gave a hysteric but joyful sniff, and her eyes looked quite moist with delight.

"It ain't nothin' but flannin, an' the flannin ain't new; but I wanted to give yer somethin' an' I made it of nights. I knew yer could pretend it was satin with diamond pins in. I tried to when I was makin' it. The card, miss," rather doubtfully; "'t warn't wrong of me to pick it up out o' the dust-bin, was it? Miss 'Meliar' had throwed it away. I hadn't no card o' my own, an' I knowed it wouldn't be a proper presink if I didn't pin a card on—so I pinned Miss 'Meliar's.'"

Sara flew at her and hugged her. She could not have told herself or anyone else why there was a lump in her throat.

"Oh, Becky!" she cried out, with a queer little laugh, "I love you, Becky—I do, I do!"

"Oh, miss!" breathed Becky. "Thank yer, miss, kindly; it ain't good enough for that. The—the flannin wasn't new."

Happy Birthday 35

What Do You Get for
the Street That Has
Everything?

Approximately 100,000 partygoers attended the world's largest birthday party, in Aberdeen, Scotland, on July 24, 1994. The party celebrated the 200th birthday of Union Street, the city's main thoroughfare.

Happy Birthday 37

Birthday Offering.

This is my birthday offering
I'm sure you'll love them well—
And which one is the dearest
I know you cannot tell.

Gifts make friendship last longer.

—Danish proverb

Happy Birthday 39

Infant Sorrow

My mother groand! my father wept.
Into the dangerous world I leapt;
Helpless, naked, piping loud:
Like a fiend hid in a cloud.

Struggling in my father's hands:
Striving against my swadling bands:
Bound and weary I thought best
To sulk upon my mother's breast.

—William Blake

Happy Birthday 41

Carmelina Fedele of Aversa, Italy, gave birth to a twenty-two-pound, eight-ounce boy in September 1955.

He was the heaviest surviving baby ever recorded.

Happy Birthday 43

Your birthday is the one day of the year where you can successfully exert a bit of leverage.

—Merrill Markoe

. . . I've never felt old. I truly believe there isn't anything I've done in life that I can't do better right now.

—T. Boone Pickens, seventy-two years old

Mother's Birthday

Up the stairs very gently we creep,
At the door very softly we knock,
And we wonder if Mother's asleep
(We were dressed before seven o'clock).
If she thinks it's the letters or tea
What a splendid surprise it will be!

For it's only the children—it's us,
Who are standing outside at her door.
There is Sylvia and Peggy and Gus,
We three, and the baby makes four—
And we're bringing her flowers to say
"Many happy returns of the day!"

—Githa Sowerby

Who Gets to Blow
out the Candles?

In the eighteenth century, a peasant woman from Shuya, Russia, gave birth to sixty-nine children consisting of sixteen sets of twins, seven sets of triplets, and four sets of quadruplets.

From *Two Years in the Forbidden City*
by Princess Der Ling

A few days before my own birthday came around, the tenth day of the fifth moon, [the head eunuch] informed me that the custom of the Court was to make a present to Her Majesty and said that the present should take the form of fruit, cakes, etc., so I ordered eight boxes of different kinds.

Early in the morning I put on full Court dress, and made myself look as nice as possible and went to wish Her Majesty good morning. When she had finished dressing, the eunuchs brought in the presents and, kneeling, I presented them to Her Majesty, bowing to the ground nine times. She thanked me and wished me a happy birthday. She then made me a present of a pair of sandalwood bracelets, beautifully carved, also a few rolls of brocade silk. She also informed me that she had ordered some macaroni in honor of my birthday. This macaroni is called (Chang Shou Me'en) long life macaroni. This was the custom. I again bowed and thanked her for her kindness and thoughtfulness. After bowing to the Young Empress and receiving in return two pairs of shoes and several embroidered neckties, I returned to my room, where I found presents from all the Court ladies.

Altogether I had a very happy birthday.

What a

Difference a

Year Can

Make

In Korea, a baby is not considered "fully human" until its first birthday celebration, called a *tol* (tuhl). In Japan, however, babies are considered one year old at birth.

Happy Birthday 55

One cannot have too large a party.

—Jane Austen

Happy Birthday 57

Party Games

Although magicians, clowns, and dance bands are all great ways to entertain your guests at a party, games are still the most popular form of amusement at any birthday bash. Games help make a party fun and memorable and they are the perfect excuse for adults to let their hair down and act like kids again.

Wishes and Won'ts
You'll need five or more players, paper, and pencils.

Each player is assigned a number by the host. Write your number, but not your name, on a piece of paper. Then write down three secret wishes, such as, "I've always wanted my own horse"; "I've always wanted to go sky-diving"; and "I've always wanted a pink jeep."

Then list three things you'd never do, such as: "I'd never go bungee-jumping"; "I'd never eat insects"; and "I'd never swim with sharks." After ten minutes, the papers are collected and redistributed. Listen as the other players read the list they have been given. Then guess which player each list belongs to and write down that player's number. The player who correctly guesses the greatest number of people wins.

The game works best if all players are honest about their wishes and won'ts—

imaginative but honest. It's interesting how often couples will fail to identify each other: "I never knew you wanted to go sky-diving!"

Sardines
You'll need three or more players.

Sardines is a classic childhood game similar to hide-and-seek. One party guest has three minutes to hide—either in the house or on the grounds. When the time's up, everyone goes off in search of the guest. But, unlike hide-and-seek, in Sardines, when you find the hidden players, you don't reveal their hiding places. Instead, you hide also . . . then wait for everyone else to find (and hide) along with you. When the last person finds the group, that person must then go off and hide, while the others wait three minutes, starting the game all over again.

Crab Soccer

You'll need two or more players, a ball, and space to play.

Crab soccer is a great outdoor game for kids and adults. All you need is a grassy yard, a ball, such as a soccer ball or basketball, and two or more people, divided into equal teams. Like regular soccer, the object of the game is to kick the ball into the other person's/team's net. You can set up sticks or place rocks to determine goal boundaries if you don't have actual nets. Participants get down on all fours—crab-style, propped up on hands and legs, backside facing the ground—and kick the ball with their feet.

Decide which team should go first, then begin the game in the center of the playing field. Pushing and kicking of other players is prohibited, as is getting "out of position"—players must remain in crab-form throughout the game.

Either play against the clock, in which case the most points in fifteen minutes wins, or for points, in which case six points wins. The most difficult aspect of this game is trying not to laugh as you crawl and squirm around the playing field!

The Dictionary Game
You'll need three or more players, paper, pencil, and a dictionary.

This game can be played with individual players or in teams, depending on the number of people participating. Everyone gets a pencil and paper, and the first player—the caller—also gets a dictionary. The caller chooses an obscure word, reveals to the other players what that word is, and writes down the actual meaning of the word on a piece of paper.

Players must reveal beforehand if they know the meaning of the word, and another word will be chosen. Everyone then writes down a spoof meaning of the word and gives them to the caller, who reads all the definitions, including the correct one.

Players, in turns, must then guess which definition is true. Those who guess correctly receive two points. Players whose spoof definitions are picked by other players as the correct answer receive one point for each pick. Whoever gets the most points wins. Choose either a time limit or point limit (twenty points) to determine the winner.

Mirth prolongeth life, and causeth health.

—Nicholas Udall

Louisa May Alcott

Louisa May Alcott (1832–1888), the well-known author of several novels, most notably the beloved *Little Women*, kept a diary throughout her life that, among other topics, chronicled her family life.

October 8, 1843

When I woke up, the first thought I got was, "It's Mother's birthday: I must be very good." I ran and wished her a happy birthday, and gave her my kiss. After breakfast we gave her our presents. I had a moss cross and a piece of poetry for her. We did not have any school, and played in the woods and got red leaves. In the evening we danced and sung, and I read a story about "Contentment."

—Diary entry, Louisa May Alcott

Happy Birthday 67

Her birthdays were always important to her; for being a born lover of life, she would always keep the day of her entrance into it as a very great festival indeed.

—Elizabeth Goudge

Happy Birthday 69

Growth . . . exciting . . . dynamic
and alarming. Growth of the soul,
growth of the mind. . . .

—Vita Sackville-West

Happy Birthday 71

From *The Birthday of the Infanta*
by Oscar Wilde

It was the birthday of the Infanta. She was just twelve years of age, and the sun was shining brightly in the gardens of the palace.

Although she was a real Princess and the Infanta of Spain, she had only one birthday every year, just like the children of quite poor people, so it was naturally a matter of great importance to the whole country that she should have a really fine day for the occasion. And a really fine day it certainly was. The tall striped tulips stood straight up upon their stalks, like long rows of soldiers, and looked defiantly across the grass at the roses, and said: "We are quite as splendid as you are now." The purple butterflies fluttered about with gold dust on their wings, visiting each flower in turn; the little lizards crept out of the crevices of the wall, and lay basking in the white glare; and the pomegranates split and cracked with the heat, and showed their bleeding red hearts. Even the pale yellow lemons, that hung in such profusion from the mouldering trellis and along the dim arcades, seemed to have caught a richer colour from the wonderful sunlight, and the magnolia trees opened their great globe-like blossoms of folded ivory, and filled the air with a sweet heavy perfume.

The little Princess herself walked up and down the terrace with her companions, and played at hide and seek round the stone vases and the old moss-grown statues. On ordinary days she was only allowed to play with children of her own rank, so she had always to play alone, but her birthday was an exception, and the King had given orders that she was to invite any of her young friends whom she liked to come and amuse themselves with her. There was a stately grace about these slim Spanish children as they glided about, the boys with their large-plumed hats and short fluttering cloaks, the girls holding up the trains of their long brocaded gowns, and shielding the sun from their eyes with huge fans of black and silver. But the Infanta was the most graceful of all, and the most tastefully attired, after the somewhat cumbrous fashion of the day. Her robe was of grey satin, the skirt and the wide puffed sleeves heavily embroidered with silver, the stiff corset studded with rows of fine pearls. Two tiny slippers with big pink rosettes peeped out beneath her dress as she walked. Pink and pearl was her great gauze fan, and in her hair, which like an aureole of faded gold stood out stiffly round her pale little face, she had a beautiful white rose.

In Mexico, birthday parties usually feature a piñata, a decorated papier-mâché container typically shaped like an animal that is filled with candies, small toys, and coins. The piñata hangs from the ceiling and blindfolded children attempt to break it with a stick. When it breaks, everyone scrambles for the prizes.

Happy Birthday 75

As one grows older one climbs with surprising strides.

—George Sand

Happy Birthday 77

Flow, flow, flow, the current of life is ever onward . . .

—Kobo Daishi

Don't seek to recall yesterday that
   is past
Nor repine for tomorrow which has
   not yet come;
Don't build your hopes on the past
   or the future.
Be happy now and don't live on
   wind.

—Omar Khayyám

Thou wind of joy, and youth, and
   love;
Spirit of the new-wakened year!
The sun in his blue realm above
Smooths a bright path when thou
   art here.

—William Cullen Bryant

Happy Birthday 83

What's in a Name?

Today, ten of the most popular girls' names in the United States are:

Brittany

Ashley

Jessica

Amanda

Sarah

Megan

Samantha

Stephanie

Caitlin

Katherine

Today, ten of the most popular boys' names in the United States are:

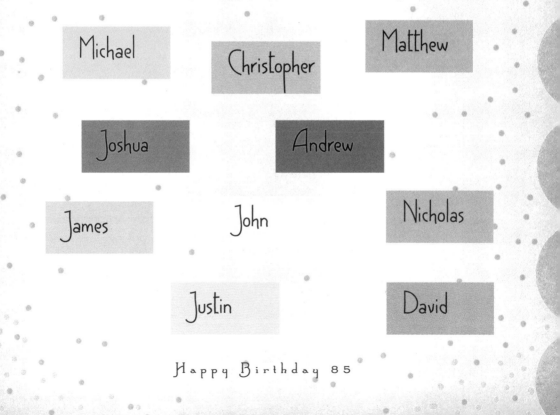

Michael

Christopher

Matthew

Joshua

Andrew

James

John

Nicholas

Justin

David

Happy Birthday 85

Fifty years ago, the ten favorite girls' names were:

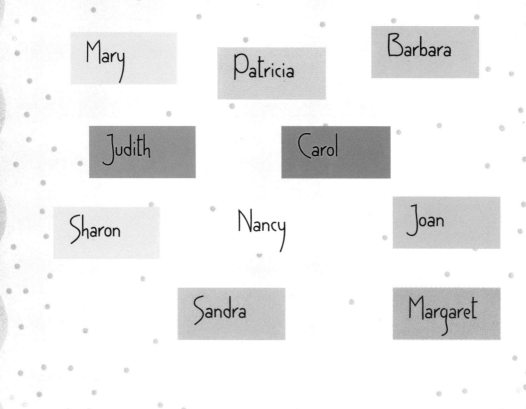

Mary

Patricia

Barbara

Judith

Carol

Sharon

Nancy

Joan

Sandra

Margaret

Fifty years ago, the ten favorite boys' names were:

Robert

James

John

William

Richard

Thomas

David

Ronald

Donald

Michael

Infant Joy

"I have no name;
I am but two days old."
What shall I call thee?
"I happy am,
Joy is my name."
Sweet joy befall thee!

Pretty joy!
Sweet joy, but two days old.
Sweet joy I call thee;
Thou dost smile,
I sing the while;
Sweet joy befall thee!

—William Blake

Happy Birthday 89

Birthdays around the World

Not all people celebrate their birthdays the same way. Some people throw lavish parties with all the fixings—cake, ice cream, balloons and decorations, games and entertainment—and others might commemorate the day with a favorite meal for dinner or a quiet evening with friends and family. People from all around the world have different ways of marking the occasion. In fact, not everyone says "Happy Birthday!"

In Brazil, they say, "Happy Anniversary!"—*Feliz Aniversario* (feh-LEEZ ah-nee-ver-SAH-ree-yoh).

Happy Birthday 91

In Canada, like the United States, the greeting is also "Happy Birthday," except in French Quebec, where it is *Bonne Fête* (bun fet).

The Chinese (Mandarin) say, "Birthday Greetings,"—*Sheng Ri Kuai Le* (shen rur kway luh).

In Ecuador, the greeting is *Feliz Dia del Santo* (feh-**LEEZ DEE**-ah del **SAHNT**-oh), or "Happy Saint's Day."

Egyptians say *Kulé Sana Winta Tayib* (koo-**LEH SAH**-na win-**TEH** tah-**YIB**), which means, "I wish you good things."

In Germany, the saying is "All is good for your birthday!" *Alles gute zum Geburtstag* (AH-les GOO-tuh tsoom geh-BURTS-tahk).

In Israel, the birthday greeting is *Yom Holedet Sameach* (yohm hoh-LEH-det sum-MAY-ahk), which means, "May the day of your birth be happy."

In the Netherlands, the Dutch saying is *Van Harte Gefeliciteerd* (vahn har-TEH geh-fell-ih-SIH-teerd)—"Hearty congratulations!"

The Sudanese have a pretty birthday greeting—*Aid Milad Jamil* (aid mih-LAHD JAH-mil), which means, "Day of birth beautiful."

Portrait of a Birthday

Bridget, anxious about aging, frets over what to do for her upcoming birthday.

Also worried about how to celebrate birthday. Size of flat and bank balance prohibits actual party. Maybe dinner party? But then would have to spend birthday slaving and would hate all guests on arrival. Could all go out for meal but then feel guilty asking everyone to pay . . .

—Helen Fielding, *Bridget Jones's Diary*

Happy Birthday 97

A Happy Birthday
to you

You grow up the day you have your first real laugh at yourself.

—Ethel Barrymore

Happy Birthday 99

Do what makes you truly happy.
There is radiance in the face of a
woman who takes joy in her life.

—Sylvie Chantecaille

What am I looking forward to?
Everything.

—Matthew Marks

Today a new sun rises for me;
everything lives, everything is
animated, everything seems to
speak to me of my passion, everything invites me to cherish it . . .

—Anne de Lenclos

From *The Inheritance*
by Louisa May Alcott

The morrow came, and Amy's seventeenth birthday was as bright and beautiful as she herself when crowned with flowers and leaning on her brother's arm. She bowed her thanks to the happy villagers, who waved their hats and drank to her health beneath the trees at the feast so bountifully spread for them.

. . . Gaily passed the day, and, as sunset faded into twilight and the villagers were gone, a thousand lights gleamed forth among the drooping trees, and music sounded from the balconies as carriage after carriage rolled through the lighted park and left its gay burden on the lawn. Soon throughout the brilliant house and grounds sounded happy voices, and gay parties wandered by.

"Is it not beautiful?" said Amy, glancing round the flower-decked saloon as she stood beside Lord Percy, her partner in the dance. "I am so happy tonight."

Your Birthstone

January
Garnet
Fortitude

February
Amethyst
Sincerity

March
Aquamarine
Truth

April
Diamond
Purity of heart

June
Pearl
Health

May
Emerald
Tranquillity

July
Ruby
Love

August
Peridot
Felicity

September
Sapphire
Wisdom

October
Opal
Hope

November
Topaz
Constancy

December
Turquoise
Mastery

Happy Birthday 109

From the Mouths of Babes

A young lady was almost overcome with joy when the occasion of her eighth birthday brought her the two gifts that she had wanted very badly, a wristwatch and a bottle of perfume. She chattered about her gifts all day long, wearying her parents of the subject. Guests were expected for dinner and her mother gently admonished her child in advance, saying, "Now, everybody knows about your presents and everybody is very happy for you. But we mustn't go on talking about them all the time."

The little girl was quiet at the table throughout most of the meal. Finally, a lull occurred in the conversation and, unable to restrain herself any longer, she burst out, "If anyone hears anything or smells anything, it's me!"

Happy Birthday 111

It is not the gift which is precious,
it is the love.

—Russian saying

Happy Birthday 113

There are three hundred and
sixty-four days when you might
get unbirthday presents . . . And
only *one* for birthday presents,
you know, there's glory for you.

—Lewis Carroll

My best
BIRTHDAY
Wishes

Annie Cooper

Annie Cooper was the youngest daughter in a large, wealthy family of boat builders from Sag Harbor, New York. From her diary entries (which she began at the age of fifteen), it seems she led a happy, carefree childhood and later, as a young adult, studied art—drawing and painting—as did many young women of her time.

December 11, 1881

Alas! alas! the 11 has arrived and crowns me 17 yrs old. I feel as though I were almost loosing [sic] my childhood, sweet childhood. And yet I do not feel so old, I feel as though I wish it were only 12 yrs. I hate to grow up. My childhood has been so sweet, I hate to part with it.

—Annie Cooper, journal entry

Happy Birthday 117

I'm at your celebrations!
How many tears! How many
exclamations!
And lifted high, how many a
brimming glass!

—Aleksándr Púshkin

I celebrate myself . . .

—Walt Whitman

Happy Birthday 121

LET THEM EAT CAKE

What's a birthday celebration without a cake (and perhaps a scoop or two of ice cream)? This wonderful tradition of marking the day with a festive party and food began thousands of years ago. The Greeks, who borrowed the Egyptian custom for celebrating birthdays, are responsible for the addition of the birthday cake to mark the day.

The writer Philochorus noted that followers of Artemis, goddess of the Moon and the hunt, commemorated her birthday on the sixth day of each month by making a cake of flour and honey. Her cake also may have been adorned with lighted candles, which represented moonlight, simulating Artemis's radiance. Like Artemis's honey concoction, these birthday recipes—some traditional, some not—are sure to be a tasty addition to any birthday gathering!

Another candle on your cake?
Well, that's no cause to pout,
Be glad that you have strength
   enough
To blow the darn thing out.

—Anonymous

Traditional Chocolate Buttermilk Cake

This classic chocolate layer cake has all the ingredients for a great party dessert . . . chocolate, chocolate, and more chocolate!

3 ounces unsweetened chocolate
½ cup butter
1 cup buttermilk
1 ½ cups sugar
3 eggs, separated
1 cup sifted flour

Topping

2 cups heavy cream
3 Tbsp. sugar
Shredded chocolate (for garnish)

Preheat oven to 325 degrees. Grease two 8-inch round cake pans and line with waxed paper that has also been buttered. Lightly dust with flour.

Using a double boiler, melt chocolate over hot water. Add butter and buttermilk and set aside. Add 1 cup of sugar to egg whites and beat until they form peaks. With remaining ½ cup of sugar, beat egg yolks until thick.

Fold chocolate mixture into egg yolks. Then alternately fold beaten egg whites (about a third at a time) and flour into chocolate mixture. Stir until smooth, but don't overmix. Divide batter between the two cake pans and bake for about 30 minutes, or until inserted knife comes out clean. Cool for 5 minutes in pans. Remove to wire rack.

For topping, whip cream with sugar. Spread about a quarter of whipped cream between the two cake layers and assemble. Finish decorating cake with remaining whipped cream. Sprinkle shredded chocolate evenly over top and sides of cake.

A Recipe for the Ages

Ice cream, often served with birthday cake, was created 4,000 years ago in China. The original recipe for ice cream, a favored dish of China's nobility, consisted of a soft paste made of overcooked rice, spices, and milk, which was packed in snow to freeze. The ancient Chinese also made fruit ices by mixing fruit pulp or fruit juice with snow.

We are always the same age inside.

—Gertrude Stein

"1-2-3" Ice-cream Cake

Did you just find out it's your dinner guest's birthday, and you don't have a cake on hand to celebrate? Quick, sneak into the kitchen and grab some cookies and ice cream for this fast, fun ice-cream cake.

Take a half-gallon block of ice cream, unwrap it, and cover with lady fingers or another favorite kind of cookie. Place back in freezer until ready to use. Cut in slices and serve.

According to the International Ice Cream Association, the United States consumes more ice cream (including frozen yogurt, ices, sorbet, and sherbet) than any other country.

Classic Cupcakes

Children, always on the go, will love these cupcakes because they're portable and kids can eat them anywhere. And they can be decorated to suit any party theme, whether it's the circus, the zoo, or even the color blue!

1 ¼ cups flour
2 tsp. baking powder
⅛ tsp. salt
¼ tsp. cream of tartar
½ cup plus 2 Tbsp. milk
1 ½ tsp. vanilla
¾ stick of butter or margarine
⅔ cup sugar
2 large eggs
1 can frosting, any flavor

Preheat oven to 400 degrees. In a large bowl combine flour, baking powder, salt, and cream of tartar. In another bowl, mix milk and vanilla together. Using a standard-size, 12-cup muffin tin, line the cups with paper liners or grease with butter.

In another large bowl, beat butter at high speed until soft. Add sugar and continue beating until mixture is well blended and fluffy. Then add eggs, beating until they are well blended. Add half of dry ingredients and half of milk/vanilla mixture and mix at medium speed for approximately 30 seconds. Add remaining ingredients and beat until blended.

Drop batter into muffin tin cups with a large spoon until they are almost full. Just as you put the cupcakes in the oven, lower the temperature to 375. Bake for about 30 minutes or until a toothpick comes out clean. Cool cupcakes in pan for 15 minutes. Remove them from tin, finish cooling them on a wire rack, and frost the cupcakes. Makes 12 kids very happy.

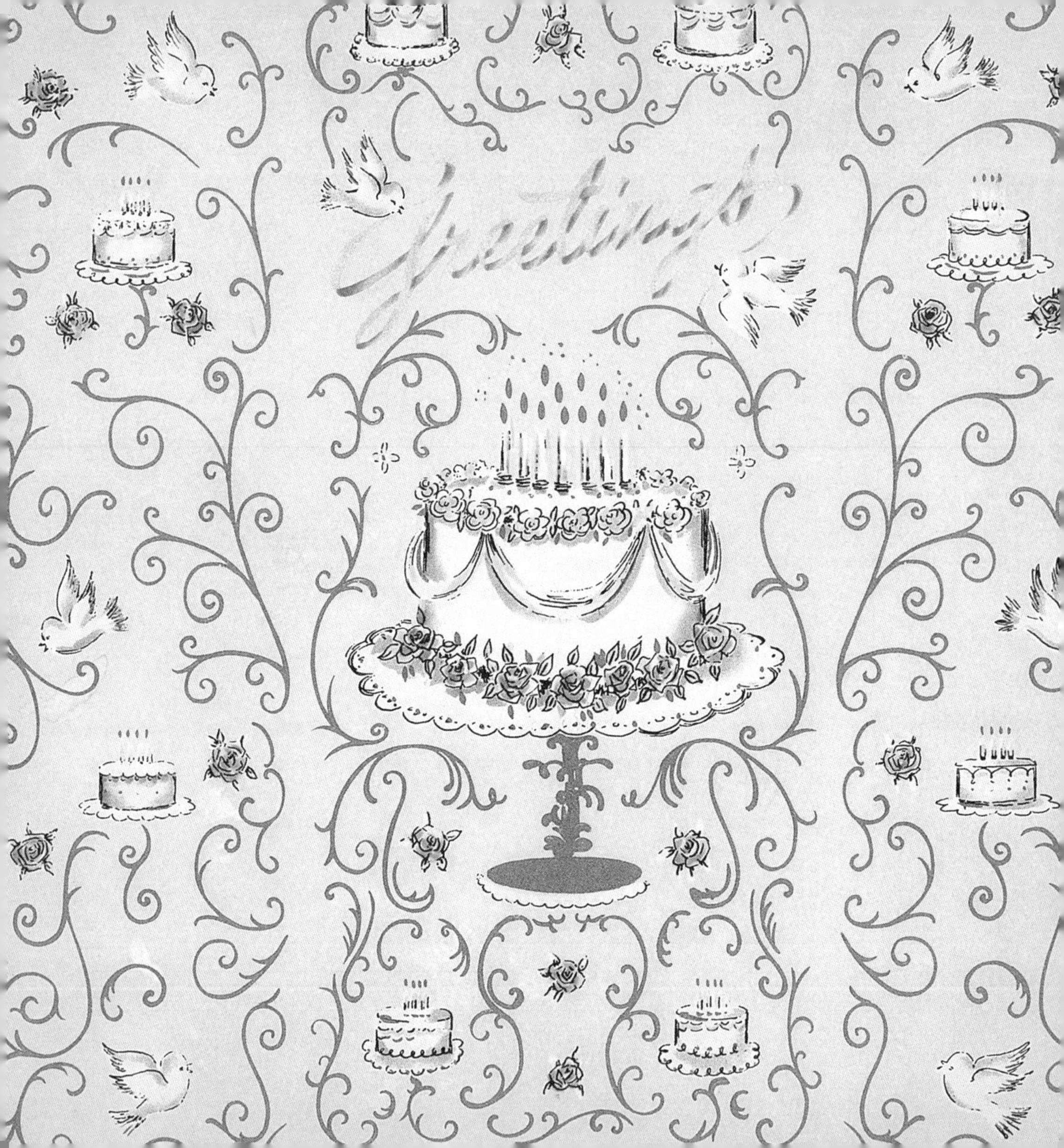
Greetings

You eat your fill—for what else
could you wish?

—Nguyên Dinh Chieu

Pizza Cookie

This big chocolate chip cookie is decorated to resemble a pizza pie, and it's as fun to make as it is to eat. So why not ask your guests to bring a favorite topping and help decorate the "pie" as part of the festivities?

"Pizza" dough

¾ cup butter, softened
¾ cup sugar
½ cup brown sugar
2 eggs
1 ½ tsp. vanilla or almond extract
1 ⅔ cups flour
   ½ tsp. baking soda
     ¼ tsp. salt
       ½ cup semisweet chocolate chips
       ½ cup white chocolate chips or butterscotch chips

"Pizza" toppings

⅔ cup seedless red jam (strawberry or raspberry), or vanilla icing mixed
    with red food coloring (for the "sauce")
2 Tootsie Rolls, cut into ¼-inch slices
4 ounces white chocolate, shaved
2 Twizzler sticks, cut into ¼-inch pieces

Place an upside-down muffin tin in a preheated oven (375 degrees). In a
large bowl, combine butter, sugar, and brown sugar until smooth. Beat in
eggs and vanilla or almond extract. In a separate bowl, stir flour, baking
soda, and salt together. Combine flour mixture with butter/egg batter and
stir until smooth. Add chocolate and butterscotch chips.

Evenly pat dough around a 13-inch greased and floured pizza pan. Leave
room near the edge for cookie to spread. Place pizza pan on top of muffin
tin so when it's done, you can lift it from the bottom and not touch the
cookie.

Bake the pizza cookie for 20 minutes or until a knife comes out clean.
Spread jam or icing on top of dough and sprinkle with Tootsie Roll slices
or shaved white chocolate or Twizzler sticks or other toppings of your
choice. Cool on wire rack. Cut into 16 slices.

The world's oldest piece of cake is on exhibit at the

Alimentarium Food Museum in Vevey, Switzerland.

The cake, which had been sealed and vacuum-packed,

was discovered in the grave of an ancient Egyptian,

Pepionkh, who lived around 2200 B.C.

I've always roared with laughter when they say life begins at forty. That's the funniest remark ever. The day I was born was when life began for me.

—Bette Davis

Light and Airy Chiffon Cake

This delightfully light cake is perfect for a friend's or family member's birthday when there's just a handful of people partaking in a casual celebration. Serve with afternoon tea and a gift or two.

2 ¼ cups all-purpose flour
3 tsp. baking powder
¼ tsp. salt
1 ½ cups granulated sugar
½ cup vegetable oil
¾ cup orange juice
1 ½ tsp. grated orange peel
7 egg yolks
    1 tsp. vanilla
       7 egg whites
         ½ tsp. cream of tartar

Grease *only* the bottom (or use a piece of waxed paper) of a 10-inch round tube pan with removable bottom or two 9-inch layer cake pans. Lightly dust greased pan bottom with flour. In a large bowl mix flour, baking powder, salt, and 1 cup of sugar. Make a well in center of dry ingredients and add oil, orange juice, orange peel, egg yolks, and vanilla. Mix (with electric mixer) at low speed until ingredients are completely blended.

In separate bowl, beat egg whites until they are frothy; add cream of tartar and mix until peaks form. Add remaining sugar while continuing to mix. Beat until soft peaks form, but do not overbeat. Gently add egg whites, one third at a time, to cake batter.

After all ingredients are blended, pour batter into baking pan and smooth the top. Bake at 325 degrees for approximately one hour, or until cake is lightly browned or a knife comes out clean. Don't overbake. Remove from oven immediately when done. Allow to cool completely before taking out of pan. Use a serrated knife to cut cake. Serve with ice cream, whipped cream, or fruit.

What gift is there that equals the
gift of food!

—Indian saying

Crunchy Carrot Cake

Because this carrot cake is a nice alternative to more traditional birthday cakes, the yummy leftovers, which are so un-birthdaylike, might not remind you that you just turned another year older!

4 eggs
¾ cup brown sugar
2 sticks (1 cup) butter or margarine, melted
½ cup orange juice
2 cups flour
2 tsp. baking powder
1 tsp. nutmeg
1 ½ tsp. cinnamon
1 ⅔ cups grated carrot
½ cup semisweet chocolate chips
½ cup raisins
½ cup walnuts, chopped
1 can vanilla icing (optional)

Preheat oven to 350 degrees. Beat eggs in a large bowl, gradually adding brown sugar, melted butter or margarine, and orange juice. In a separate bowl, stir flour, baking powder, and spices together. Add egg mixture to dry ingredients and stir. Last, add grated carrot, chocolate chips, raisins, and walnuts and mix together. Grease and lightly flour a tube pan.

Pour batter into tube pan and bake for 1 hour or until knife comes out clean. Cool on wire rack. If desired, when cool, spread on vanilla icing.

The

First

Birthday

Party

The first recorded birthday celebrations were those of the early pharaohs (Egyptian kings), around 3000 B.C. Parties were luxurious feasts in which all members of a royal household were invited, including servants and slaves.

Birthday Popcorn Cake

Sure to be a favorite with children, this popcorn cake is fast, easy, and—as the kids at the party will no doubt tell you—totally awesome!

6 qts. popped popcorn
1 lb. gumdrops
1 ½ cups peanuts
1 large bag of marshmallows
½ cup salad oil
¼ cup butter or margarine

Combine popcorn, gumdrops, and peanuts in bowl. Melt marshmallows, oil, and butter together over low heat and mix together well. Pour this mixture over popcorn mixture and stir together in a well-greased angel food cake pan. Cool 10 minutes and remove from pan. Decorate with additional gumdrops and candies.

You have wine and food;
Why not play daily on your lute,
That you may enjoy yourself now
And lengthen your days? . . .

—Anonymous Chinese ode

Coconut Triple Layer Cake

Won't you be the hit of the party (next to the birthday guest, of course) when the lights are turned on and you yell "Surprise!" while holding this sky-high, festive, triple-layer cake. After the shock of the surprise wears off, there's sure to be a big smile on the face of the guest of honor when she realizes this cake is for her!

3 cups cake flour
2 tsp. baking powder
½ tsp. salt
1 cup butter or margarine, softened
2 cups sugar
4 eggs
1 tsp. vanilla
1 cup milk
5 ounces flaked coconut
1 ½ cans vanilla frosting

Butter three 8-inch or two 9-inch round layer cake pans and lightly dust with flour. In a large bowl, mix flour, baking powder, and salt. In a separate bowl, beat butter or margarine, sugar, eggs, and vanilla with an electric mixer at high speed.

Slowly mix flour mixture and milk together with electric mixer at low speed. Add butter mixture and blend until smooth. Pour batter into greased baking pans. Bake at 350 degrees for about 30 minutes or until centers bounce back when lightly touched. Cool on wire racks for 15 minutes, then remove from pans. Spread frosting on top of each layer, sprinkle with coconut, then put layers together. Frost remainder of cake and sprinkle sides and top with coconut. Makes one 8-inch triple-layer cake or one 9-inch double-layer cake.

The largest cake ever made—weighing 128,238 pounds, 8 ounces—was baked to celebrate the 100th birthday of Fort Payne, Alabama. The Alabama-shaped cake was made by a local bakery, EarthGrains, in 1989. The first piece was cut by local centenarian Ed Henderson.

I am in the prime of senility.

—Joel Chandler Harris

Apple Walnut Chocolate Torte

If you're cooking a special dinner for someone's birthday, consider serving this delicious torte for dessert. Served with coffee and memories of birthdays past, this torte will cause guests to clamor for seconds.

4 apples
1 ½ cups finely chopped walnuts
¼ cup flour
2 ounces bittersweet chocolate
¾ cup sugar
5 large eggs, separated
3 tsp. kirschwasser (cherry brandy) or Calvados (apple brandy)

Preheat oven to 325 degrees. Grease one 9-inch round cake pan and line with buttered waxed paper. Lightly dust paper with flour.

Core, peel, and grate apples. Mix apples with walnuts and flour and set aside.

Using a double boiler, melt chocolate over hot water. With ½ cup of sugar, beat egg whites until they form peaks. Then beat egg yolks with remaining ¼ cup of sugar until thick. Mix melted chocolate with egg yolks. Fold beaten egg whites and apple/walnut mixture into chocolate mixture. Stir until smooth, but don't overmix.

Pour batter into cake pan and bake for approximately 1 hour or until inserted knife comes out clean. Cool for approximately 10 minutes, then remove to a piece of corrugated cardboard (cut round, about the size of cake). Sprinkle torte with sugar, then wrap in plastic. Let torte sit in refrigerator for at least 10 hours before serving. Sprinkle 3 teaspoons of kirschwasser or Calvados over torte. Makes 10–16 servings.

A very merry, dancing,
    drinking,
Laughing, quaffing, and
    unthinking time.

—John Dryden

Lemon Squares

If you've been asked to bring a dish to a desserts-only birthday party, then whip up these tasty lemon squares, which are guaranteed to stand out from the crowd.

1 cup flour stirred with ⅛ tsp. salt
½ cup sugar
½ cup (1 stick) unsalted butter, cut into ½-inch pieces

Topping

3 eggs
⅔ cup sugar
1 ½ Tbsp. flour
1 ¼ tsp. grated lemon rind
⅓ cup fresh lemon juice
Confectioners' sugar

Preheat oven to 375 degrees. Grease and lightly flour a 9- x 9-inch baking dish. In large bowl, mix flour and sugar together.

Add butter and mix until it clumps. Evenly pat dough over bottom of baking dish. Bake for approximately 15 minutes, or until top appears dry and its edges are lightly browned. Cool on wire rack, while still in dish. Reduce oven temperature to 350.

To make topping, combine eggs, sugar, flour, lemon rind, and lemon juice in bowl or food processor and mix until well blended. Pour mixture over dough in baking dish. Bake for approximately 15–17 minutes or until top is dry. Do not overcook. Let lemon "cake" cool on wire rack for an hour. Sprinkle with 2–3 tablespoons confectioners' sugar. Cut into squares. Makes approximately 25 servings.

Arise and eat bread, and let thine heart be merry.

—Jezebel

Banana Nut Layer Cake

Seconds, anyone? It will come as no surprise that this fabulous classic-with-a-twist banana layer cake is eaten up in record time. It's so delicious, you should have made two.

2 ⅓ cups cake flour
2 ½ tsp. baking powder
½ tsp. baking soda
¼ tsp. salt
½ tsp. ground cinnamon
¼ tsp. nutmeg
½ cup buttermilk
1 cup ripe bananas, mashed (about 2 medium bananas)
   ½ cup butter or margarine
     1 ¼ cups sugar
    2 eggs
     ¼ tsp. vanilla
     1 cup chopped walnuts
     1 can banana, rum butter, or vanilla frosting

Butter two 9-inch round layer cake pans and dust lightly with flour. In large mixing bowl, combine flour, baking powder, baking soda, salt, cinnamon, and nutmeg. In separate bowl, stir buttermilk and mashed bananas together.

Beat butter or margarine, sugar, and eggs with electric mixer at high speed until well blended. Stir together flour and banana mixtures and beat by hand until smooth. Add vanilla and ¼ cup of chopped nuts and blend. Pour mixture into baking pans. Bake at 350 degrees for about 30 minutes, or until centers bounce back when lightly pressed. Cool on wire racks for 15 minutes, then remove from pans.

Put layers together with icing, then frost remainder of cake. Press remaining chopped nuts onto sides and top of cake. Makes one double-layer cake.

A WHAT'S YOUR SIGN?

lthough no one really knows how or why, many personality traits can be predicted according to your birthday. Are you a bold Sagittarius, a disciplined Capricorn, or an earthy Taurus? Do you love to wear the color purple, swim in the ocean, or entertain friends with elaborate parties?

Your birth sign influences everything you do from your tastes to your behavior to your choice of careers and love partners. Every sign in the zodiac is as unique and complex as each individual. Read on and discover some surprises about your friends, your family, and perhaps even yourself!

Aries

March 21–April 20

Aries, like newborn babies, are constantly aware and enthralled by themselves and the world around them. The Ram is enthusiastic, exuberant, passionate, and often self-centered—traits usually associated with youth. Ruled by Mars, the planet of war, Aries is symbolized by the Ram, which figures in ancient mythology as a symbol of sacrifice. Aries loves a good fight—and the only way to win an argument with the Ram is to give in. Once Aries get their way, the lighter, sweeter side of the Aries temperament will shine through. For the Ram, wild mood swings are normal, and Aries seem incapable of even remembering past bad behavior, especially if it conflicts with their present mood. The Ram lives strictly for today.

Aries can be great conversationalists and creative storytellers. Like children who can amuse themselves for hours by counting their fingers and toes, Aries are forever fascinated with *themselves!* Rams despise boredom and routine: They must constantly seek challenges to avoid depression. There is also the danger of making spontaneous—and often disastrous—changes in work and family life, just to shake things up.

The Ram possesses superior athletic prowess and high energy, but nervous exhaustion can cause Aries to literally burn out. Lots of rest and plenty of protein and carbohydrates will help keep Rams well balanced and healthy.

Aries is associated with Tuesday and rules the head and face. The Ram's lucky number is five. The best color for the Ram is red, and the Ram's metal is iron. Flowers and plants associated with Aries are thistle, holly, poppy, and anemone.

Famous Aries

Leonardo da Vinci, painter and inventor
J. P. Morgan, financier and art collector
Harry Reasoner, TV journalist
Charlie Chaplin, actor
Ellen Barkin, actress
Annie Sullivan, Helen Keller's teacher
Tama Janowitz, novelist
Ethel Kennedy, wife of Robert Kennedy
Charles Baudelaire, French poet
Billie Holiday, jazz singer
David Letterman, talk show host
Oleg Cassini, fashion designer

Taurus

April 21–May 21

Taurus, ruled by the planet Venus, is symbolized by the Bull. Those born under this sign have a heightened sensuality, an innate sense of beauty, and possess great strength. The Bull is also gentle, patient, romantic, stable, loving, and stubborn. There's a good reason Taurus is associated with the Bull—Tauruses can be extremely bullheaded—to the point that once they have made up their minds, that is that! Although usually quite placid, Bulls keep their anger bottled up until it explodes. Luckily, such explosions are few and far between. Most Bulls live much of their lives without ever experiencing the full depth of their anger. In fact, Tauruses tend to be steady and docile and deeply loving, even if they rarely show it.

Bulls excel at work, and their output is steady and always top quality. They're effective organizers and good at meeting (and beating!) deadlines, and they will work overtime without objection. The Bull does have a tendency to be a little shy at times. If someone wants to get to know a Taurus, he will need to take a chance and give the Bull a call. The Bull will likely be a very faithful friend or an affectionate, giving lover.

This earth sign also enjoys gardening and a comfortable home. In fact, farming, raising plants, and breeding stock are all good career choices for Taurus.

They also make excellent chefs, composers, writers, and artists. Taurus, who is associated with Friday, rules the throat and neck. Bulls' lucky number is six, and their colors are pastels of all shades. Their metal is copper, and the plants and flowers that relate to Taurus are the daisy, larkspur, rose, columbine, lily, and foxglove.

Famous Tauruses

Theo van Gogh, Vincent's brother
Sugar Ray Robinson, boxer
Golda Meir, Israeli prime minister
Audrey Hepburn, actress
Harry S. Truman, U.S. president
Candice Bergen, actress
Ricky Nelson, singer
Fred Astaire, dancer and actor
Martha Graham, dancer and choreographer
George Carlin, comedian
Malcolm X, activist and writer
Nora Ephron, film director and novelist

Gemini

May 22–June 21

Geminis, also known as the Twins, reflect the duality of the sign under which they were born, often appearing to be two people. Ruled by Mercury, Gemini is named after the ancient Roman god of commerce, eloquence, and travel, who served as messenger of the gods. The very embodiment of diplomacy, Geminis possess wit, charm, and a brilliant mastery of language (Gemini is also the sign of communication). Versatile, forthright, and sometimes superficial, Gemini is an innovative thinker and energetic explorer.

However, it can often be difficult to find the true Gemini underneath the sleek exterior. Although the Twins can easily entice others into disclosing all, they also use these same bells and whistles to conceal their true self from the world. Gemini also is unpredictable and capable of quickly shifting moods and attitudes, a clear reflection of their dual nature. The Twins also enjoy multi-tasking as opposed to working for hours at one job, which is sheer torture for them. Their quick and curious minds often distract them from the task at hand, causing them to jump from one project to the next at breakneck speed.

The average Gemini has a tendency to walk, talk, eat, and think faster than most people. So the Twins need plenty of rest and nourishment to replenish the considerable energy they expend each day. A varied exercise program, preferably outdoors in fresh air, and a healthy diet can be most beneficial.

Gemini rules the shoulders, arms, hands, lungs, and nerves and is linked with Wednesday. The Twins' lucky number is seven, yellow is their color, and mercury is their metal. The plants and flowers associated with Gemini are ferns, myrtle, jasmine, and grafted trees.

Famous Geminis

John F. Kennedy, U.S. president
Annette Bening, actress
Peter the Great, Russian tsar
Walt Whitman, poet
Peter Carl Fabergé, Russian jeweler
Marilyn Monroe, actress
Colleen McCullough, novelist
Josephine Baker, dancer and entertainer
Bill Moyers, journalist
Nathan Hale, American revolutionary
Paul Gauguin, painter
Louis Gossett Jr., actor

Cancer

June 22–July 23

The home and family are the very core of existence for those born under the sign of Cancer the Crab. True homebodies, Cancers want to take care of their loved ones with good advice and good food. For the Crab, being well fed means being satisfied and content. Happily dishing up second and third helpings is Cancer's way of dishing out love and affection. Though they prefer the four walls of their comfortable homes, they do have an ambitious side, though they rarely seek recognition. Of course, a career in health, education, or child care appeals to the caring Crab, who is protective, nurturing, and empathetic.

Ruled by the Moon, Cancer has as many moods as the Moon has faces, and is capable of going from laughter to tears in a New York minute. Since the Moon also represents cycles, Cancers may find themselves affected by changes in the seasons and weather, and can easily become depressed. For this moody sign, laughter is the best medicine.

As a water sign, Cancer enjoys water sports of all kinds, including swimming, water skiing, and scuba diving. They also tend to like boats—from cruise ships to canoes—and can fish for hours. Crabs love movies and the theater, though they prefer staying in to going out. And with their fondness for the past, they will probably choose a movie that's a classic, such as *Gone With the Wind.*

Cancer, who is linked with Monday, rules the chest, breasts, and digestive system. Their lucky number is two, and light blue is their color, as is silver, which is also their metal. Plants and flowers associated with Cancer are the hazelnut tree, geranium, water lily, and all white flowers.

Famous Cancers

Abigail Van Buren and Ann Landers, twin sisters and advice columnists
Gina Lollobrigida, actress
Phineas T. Barnum, circus founder
Frida Kahlo, painter
Sylvester Stallone, actor
Marc Chagall, painter
Barbara Cartland, author
Tom Hanks, actor
Legs Diamond, gangster
David Dinkins, New York mayor
David Brinkley, TV journalist
Kristy Yamaguchi, ice skater
Julius Caesar, Roman ruler

Leo

Dignity, pride, and strength describe Leo the Lion. Those born under this sign are dynamic and charismatic, and possess a natural talent for leadership. Leo is ruled by the Sun, the center of the solar system and giver of life. And like the Sun, Leos shed their light and warmth generously on those around them. In return, Leos ask only one thing: that they be the center of their universe—the biggest and brightest star around! Because Leos love to be the center of attention, they tend to spend a lot of time primping and posing in front of the mirror in preparation for the spotlight.

Therefore, it's no surprise that Leos love to entertain. An outgoing and accommodating host, the Lion tries to make each and every guest feel welcome and comfortable. But beneath Leos' confident exterior may lurk self-doubts or fears of rejection, which may cause them to indulge their taste for melodrama. For Leos, expressing their emotions, whether positive or negative, is essential to their daily routine. On the other hand, the Lion is good-natured, creative, and generous.

Because Leos love an audience, a career as an actor or politician will appeal to them. They also like to be in positions of authority—their ambition, enthusiasm, courage, dramatic flair, talent for organization, and leadership make them perfect candidates for public office.

Leo, who is associated with Sunday, rules the heart, spine, and back. Leo's lucky number is nineteen, and red, orange, gold, and yellow are Leo's colors. Gold is the Lion's metal, and plants and flowers linked with Leo are the yellow lily, poppy, sunflower, and marigold.

Famous Leos

Whitney Houston, singer
Jimmy Dean, singer
Alex Haley, writer
Cecil B. DeMille, film director
Alfred Hitchcock, film director
Annie Oakley, sharpshooter
Steve Martin, comedian and actor
Magic Johnson, basketball player
Julia Child, chef
Napoleon Bonaparte, French emperor
Madonna, singer and actress
Robert De Niro, actor
Mae West, actress
Bill Clinton, U.S. president

Virgo

August 24–September 23

Virgos epitomize virtue, devotion, and service, like the Virgin herself, under whose sign they are born. Virgos also are associated with fertility goddesses, whose nature is to enrich humankind selflessly. In both mythology and religion, the Virgin is often associated with the birth of gods and others whose offspring will have great impact on the world. For example, the Virgin Mary gave birth to Jesus.

Ruled by the planet Mercury, the Roman messenger of the gods, Virgos possess great control over their emotions and strive for excellence in all endeavors. Often perceived as uptight or repressed, Virgos are actually masters at arranging and organizing their world in order to find not just the best but the perfect solution. Improvement is the guiding force behind Virgo, who sees the world as a big machine whose parts are to be observed and analyzed so its operation can be perfected. This pursuit of excellence can make Virgo appear fussy and narrow-minded, complaining about the smallest details (and Virgos do have a hard time admitting when they are wrong), but the Virgin is simply trying to make things better. Virgo is also a devoted and loyal friend or partner, a practical and analytical thinker, and highly intelligent.

Virgo, who is linked with Wednesday, rules the stomach and intestines.

Virgos' lucky number is seven, and their colors are brown, navy, blue, violet, white, and gray. Nickel and mercury are their metals, and flowers associated with Virgo are the buttercup and forget-me-not.

Famous Virgos

Ruby Keeler, Ziegfield dancer and singer
Sean Connery, actor
Letizia Bonaparte, Napoleon's mother
Mother Teresa, nun
Man Ray, painter and photographer
Pee-wee Herman, actor
Johann Wolfgang von Goethe, poet and novelist
Scott Hamilton, ice skater
Ingrid Bergman, actress
Charlie "Bird" Parker, saxophonist
Mary Shelley, novelist
Richard Gere, actor
Charlie Sheen, actor
Queen Elizabeth I, British monarch

Libra

September 24–October 23

Those born under the sign of the Scales are constantly trying to remain in balance. Libra can be lazy or hardworking. Sometimes they're cool and uninvolved, and other times they're right in the thick of things. No single trait is allowed to dominate because it would upset Libra's delicate balancing act. The Scales are the sign of partnership, which is why Libras don't enjoy doing things alone. Hence, they often jump into early marriages to avoid loneliness.

A very social sign, Libra needs to be around other people. And for the sake of harmony and companionship, the Scales can usually find something good in everyone. In their constant quest for a harmonious life, Libras may bottle up negative feelings or conceal their true feelings from others. However, the Scales' internal balancing act ensures that repressed feelings will come out in some way—even perhaps in physical illness or unconscious actions.

Libra is ruled by the planet Venus, named after the Roman goddess of love and beauty. And because they seek beauty in all things, they want to create a peaceful, congenial environment at home. As natural-born peacemakers, Libras are attracted to jobs that allow them to mediate or negotiate, whether it be as a judge, marriage counselor, or referee. As with all areas of the Scales' life, they work to create harmony, balance, and respect in the workplace.

Libra, whose day is Friday, rules the kidneys, adrenal glands, and lumbar spine. Copper is their metal, and shades of pink are their colors. Libra's lucky number is three. Trees and flowers associated with Libra include the ash and poplar, and flowers include roses, lilies, pansies, and vines.

Famous Libras

Sting, singer
Spanky McFarland, child actor
Chubby Checker, singer
Jack LaLanne, fitness instructor
Pancho Villa, bandit
Anne Rice, novelist
Bob Geldof, musician
Jesse Jackson, political leader
Chevy Chase, actor
John Lennon, singer
Eleanor Roosevelt, first lady
Luciano Pavarotti, opera singer

Scorpio

Scorpio is ruled by mysterious Pluto, god of the underworld. And like Pluto, Scorpios likes to keep their personal force under wraps, waiting behind the scenes for the right time to make a powerful move. The symbol associated with Scorpio, the Scorpion, would rather sting itself to death than yield to a predator. Similarly, Scorpios are determined to control their own destiny at all costs. Scorpios have a tendency to keep their true nature hidden, which is one reason they are so often misunderstood. Scorpios only reveal what they want to be seen and conceal their powerfully strong emotions beneath the surface.

Like all water signs, Scorpio is concerned more with emotions than ideas, principles, or money. When they give their heart, they give it completely. If Scorpios befriend someone, they typically have made a friend for life. If not, they will not change their mind easily. And although Scorpios behave like loners, sensitive, self-possessed Scorpions long to be with others. However, they are careful to choose friends and partners who will respect their privacy and feelings.

Scorpios' self-discipline and loyalty make them ideal employees. They much prefer to work behind the scenes, for the good of the company, than to pursue personal glory. Since this sign rules banking and other professions that control money, Scorpios tend to choose careers in financial management. At home, love relationships are important to Scorpio, so they will try to preserve them at all costs. As mates, Scorpios tend to be jealous and possessive, but they are also devoted and loyal.

Scorpio, who is linked with Tuesday, rules the reproductive organs. Their colors are black and burgundy, and their metals are iron and plutonium. Plants and flowers associated with Scorpio include heather, brambles, and blackthorn.

Famous Scorpios

Indira Gandhi, Indian prime minister
Ted Turner, media mogul
Jodie Foster, actress
Calvin Klein, clothing designer
Larry King, talk show host
Voltaire, philosopher and poet
René Magritte, surrealist painter
Mariel Hemingway, actress
Sam Waterston, actor
Georgia O'Keeffe, artist
Claude Monet, painter
Aaron Copland, composer

Sagittarius

November 23–December 21

Sagittarius is the sign of exploration and expansion. Like their symbol, the Archer, Sagittarians are always aiming for a distant target. The centaur—a mythic combination of man and horse—is known for his epic adventures and vast knowledge, which was respected by princes and kings whose kingdoms prospered from the wisdom he shared with them. Like their symbol, Sagittarians also want their knowledge to benefit mankind.

Ruled by the planet Jupiter, named after the King of Roman gods, Sagittarius is confident, open, fun-loving, and both naturally giving and rebellious. The Archer tends to have a restless spirit, which may explain why this sign wants to be in the know about everything—from music to technology to current events. However, Sagittarians are easily bored and few things entice for very long. To restless Sagittarius, the chase is always more exciting than the capture.

Sagittarians also tend to be risk takers whose gambles usually pay off. On the job they need lots of variety and plenty of action as opposed to repetitive, sedentary desk jobs. If they feel challenged by their work, they are sure to excel and be happy. The Archer prefers a job that offers some benefit to others—especially children and animals—such as social workers, veterinarians, and doctors or nurses. They also make great teachers who know how to make learning fun and memorable. Careers that let them indulge their wanderlust, such as archaeology or anthropology, also appeal to their adventurous side.

Sagittarius, who is linked with Thursday, rules the hips, thighs, and liver. Purple is their color, and tin is their metal. Plants and flowers associated with the Archer are begonias, dandelions, and carnations.

Famous Sagittarians

Caroline Kennedy, attorney and daughter of JFK
Katarina Witt, ice skater
Andy Williams, singer
Little Richard, singer
Willa Cather, novelist
Ellen Burstyn, actress
Anders Celsius, astronomer
Jim Morrison, singer
Sinéad O'Connor, singer
Gustavus Adolphus the Great, Swedish king
Dame Judi Dench, actress
Emily Dickinson, poet
Chet Huntley, TV journalist

Capricorn

December 22–January 20

The Capricorn symbol is a sea goat—a goat whose tail is part fish, part serpent—which is an ancient symbol for wisdom. The fish represents the deep, watery depths and the goat represents the high, airy mountains. Those born under this sign are thought to be determined, ambitious, and industrious. They are practical and philosophical, with a tendency to conceal the emotional and sensual sides of their personality.

Ruled by Saturn, the planet of discipline, structure, and isolation, the typical Capricorn is a hard worker who slowly but surely climbs the ladder of success. Even as children, Capricorns tend to be reserved, serious, wise, and very disciplined. Luckily, as they grow older and more secure, Capricorns become more playful and fun-loving.

Often mistaken as cold and aloof, Capricorns are dignified and reserved, and they rarely reveal much about themselves to casual acquaintances. Status is very important to Capricorns, who take pride in both their career and financial standing. However, the Goat is not extravagant and dislikes waste of any kind. Capricorn derives great pleasure and security from the continuance of things. Often history buffs who cherish antiques and old buildings, tradition and family are also important to them.

Goats are associated with Wednesday and their lucky number is four. The knees, skin, bones, and teeth are all ruled by their sign. Earth tones—brown and green—as well as gray and black are good colors for the Goat. Capricorn's metal is lead, and plants and flowers associated with this sign include ivy, pansy, and amaranth.

Famous Capricorns

Crystal Gayle, country singer
Richard Nixon, U.S. president
Elvis Presley, singer and actor
David Bowie, singer
Nicolas Cage, actor
Diane Keaton, actress
Alvin Ailey, dancer and choreographer
Mel Gibson, actor
Sergio Leone, film director
Paul Revere, American revolutionary
Betsy Ross, seamstress
J. D. Salinger, novelist

Aquarius

January 21–February 19

The symbol for Aquarius, a Water Bearer pouring water from a large jug, reveals the true nature of their sign. Rather than drink the water, which symbolizes emotion in astrology, the Water Bearer brings liquid to others. Water Bearers bring sustenance to humankind because they remain emotionally detached. Ruled by the planet Uranus, Aquarius embodies the ideals of equality, freedom, and democracy, and their main goal in life is to make the world a better place.

Aquarians are great communicators who are energized by exchanging ideas with others. Immensely sociable, they tend to have friends from a variety of different backgrounds and treat everyone equally: Friends, strangers, and enemies all receive the same polite consideration.

Supportive and understanding, yet able to maintain a professional distance, Aquarians are particularly effective in helping others organize and develop their talents. Community service, teaching, and high-tech careers appeal to the Water Bearer. Aquarius is a talented, innovative thinker whose ideas are often ahead of the times. Aware of how their mental health can affect their physical well-being, Aquarians prefer to heal the body using mental techniques such as biofeedback, meditation, and mind control. Easygoing aerobics, light jogging, and racquet sports also appeal to this sign.

Aquarius is linked with Saturday, and this sign rules the shins and ankles. Aquarius's lucky number is twenty-two, and this sign's colors are pure white, electric blue, and psychedelic hues. Aquarius's metal is aluminum, and plants and flowers associated with the Water Bearer are white lilacs and orchids.

Famous Aquarians

Anita Pointer, singer
Humphrey Bogart, actor
Placido Domingo, opera singer
Princess Caroline of Monaco
George Gordon, Lord Byron; poet
Virginia Woolf, novelist
Wolfgang Amadeus Mozart, composer
Donna Reed, actress
Colette, actress and novelist
Oprah Winfrey, TV host and actress
Anton Chekhov, playwright
Rick James, singer
Langston Hughes, poet

Pisces

February 20–March 20

Pisces the Fish is ruled by the planet Neptune, named after the Roman god of the sea. Water represents the emotions in astrology, and Pisces is most at home within the fluid world of feelings. The Fish deplores monotony and restrictions and prefers a constantly evolving environment in which to grow. But because they are driven by their feelings, Pisces can experience sudden, often baffling, mood swings, which can be very draining. Time alone to rest and take a short mental vacation is recommended.

The symbol of Pisces, two fish swimming in opposite directions, hints at the duality of this sign's nature, which is often torn between the material and spiritual worlds. And as the last sign of the zodiac, the Fish contains some of all the other signs. Pisces' changeable nature gives them a chameleonlike ability to take on the qualities of other people. For instance, if Pisces dates a gourmet, the Fish will learn to cook. This is because Pisces has a tendency to respond to others rather than initiate activity. This sign is easily influenced by others—good or otherwise. To protect themselves, Pisces have learned to pull out of bad relationships and situations quickly and simply.

Most Pisces have sensitive constitutions and a low tolerance to toxins. Alcohol, drugs, cigarettes, and coffee should be avoided. Though not particularly athletic, Pisces can benefit greatly from swimming, which is a refreshing, stimulating workout ideal for the Fish. Pisces, interestingly enough, rules the feet. Pisces are linked with Thursday, and their lucky number is eleven. Aquamarine is their color and plants and flowers associated with this sign are seaweed, moss, and the water lily.

Famous Pisces

George Washington, U.S. president
Frederic Chopin, composer and pianist
Anaïs Nin, writer
Ansel Adams, photographer
Gloria Vanderbilt, heiress and designer
Kurt Cobain, singer
Alberta Hunter, jazz singer
Ron Howard, actor and film director
Tom Wolfe, novelist
Jean Harlow, actress
Alexander Graham Bell, inventor
Cyrano de Bergerac, poet and dramatist
Elizabeth Barrett Browning, poet

THE
MOST WONDERFUL DAY
OF THE YEAR

The moment after Christmas every child thinks of his birthday.

—Stephen Uys

Portrait of a Birthday

A young bride celebrates her birthday with her new husband as they settle in St. Joseph, Missouri, in 1865.

Today is my birthday. I am twenty-three years old, and little did I think on this day a year ago that my next would be celebrated with a new husband. . . . My Darling Boy awakened me this morning with a bouquet of wildflowers, still wet with rain.

—Sandra Dallas, *The Diary of Mattie Spenser*

The gift is not as precious as the thought.

—Yiddish proverb

The Little Song That Could

The song we all know as "Happy Birthday to You" is considered to be the most frequently sung music in the world. The melody was created by sisters Mildred J. Hill and Patty S. Hill in 1893, and its original title was "Good Morning to All." The song was never meant to be sung at birthday parties, but was a

morning classroom welcome to children. It became a

birthday tradition through the addition of birthday

lyrics when the song was published without permission

in a songbook in 1924.

The best birthdays of all are those
that haven't arrived yet.

—Robert Orben

Rejoice, O young man, in thy youth.

—Ecclesiastes 11:9

From the journal of
Annie Cooper

December 11, 1882

Again my birthday has rolled around & I am still spared, well & happy, no care yet hath been put upon me, I am still a happy, joyous, merry, hearty, & healthy, school girl, girl of 16 in feeling, but eighteen in years. I can't bear to think how fast my happy youth & childhood is slipping from me, that I soon will be too big to climb trees & ride horse back straddling, etc. yes, that in fact I am too big already. . . .

The eighty-ninth birthday of Colonel Harland Sanders, founder of Kentucky Fried Chicken, was the largest birthday party held for a "living guest." Some 35,000 people attended the Louisville, Kentucky, bash on September 8, 1979.

Portrait of a Birthday

Bridget comes to terms with her impending birthday.

Wish had not been born but immaculately burst into being. . . .

Hurray. Whole new positive perspective on birthday. Have been talking to Jude about book she has been reading about festivals and rites of passage in primitive cultures and am feeling happy and serene.

—Helen Fielding, *Bridget Jones's Diary*

Live as long as you may, the first twenty years are the longest half of your life.

—Robert Southey

Youth is a disease from which we all recover.

—Dorothy Fuldheim

From the diary of
Louisa May Alcott

October 8, 1868

Marmee's birthday: sixty-eight. After breakfast she found her gifts on a table in the study. Father escorted her to the big red chair, the boys prancing before blowing their trumpets, while we "girls" marched behind, glad to see the dear old Mother better and able to enjoy our little fête. The boys proudly handed her the little parcels, and she laughed and cried over our gifts and verses.

On the night of Mark Twain's birthday, some friends of the author's decided to send him a letter wishing him a happy birthday. As none of them knew where he was living at the time, they addressed the envelope: "Mark Twain, God Knows Where." A few weeks later, his friends received a note from Italy that con-sisted of two words: "He did."

One—Birthday
 more—or Ten?
Let me—choose!
Ah, Sir, None!

—Emily Dickinson

A new year is a clean slate, a chance to suck in your breath, decide all is not lost, and give yourself another chance.

—Sarah Overstreet

Birthdays
"Down
Under"

Since Australians tend to have great weather year-round, most birthday celebrations feature a barbecue. Children also enjoy a treat called Fairy Bread, buttered bread covered with colored sugar sprinkles.

From *Visions of the Prophet*
by Kahlil Gibran

It was on this very day, twenty-five years ago, that my mother brought me into the world. . . .

Twenty-five times have I orbited the sun, and I know not how many times the moon has gravitated around me. But I have not yet understood the secrets of the light nor penetrated the mysteries of darkness.

Twenty-five times have I gravitated with the moon and the sun, and with the stars, around the supreme Law of the universe. And now my soul murmurs the names of this Law, just as caves echo the waves of the sea; these caves exist only by virtue of the existence of the sea, and yet its existence is unknown to them and, without understanding the sea, they are soothed by the music of its high and low tides.

Twenty-five years ago the hand of time entered my name in the book of this strange and terrible world. And now, like a sibylline word, I symbolize sometimes nothingness and sometimes a host of things.

On this very day, every year, my soul is overwhelmed with thoughts, memories and contemplation. They halt, before my eyes, the procession of days past and show me the spirits of nights gone by; then they disperse them—just as the sun dissolves the fleecy clouds in the sky over the blue horizon—until they vanish into the recesses of my room, just as the songs of the streams die away in the deep and distant valleys.

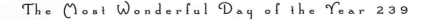

The Most Wonderful Day of the Year 239

It's a very short trip. While alive, live.

—Malcolm Forbes

happy birthday to you

Man arrives as a novice at each age of his life.

—Nicolas Chamfort

Ecuador:

Whose

Party Is It,

Anyway?

In Ecuador, the actual day of birth is not much of a celebration at all. Since most children are named for a saint, their parents throw a party for them that is much like a birthday party, but held on their saint's day. Saint's day parties typically consist of afternoon teas with elaborate cookies and hot chocolate.

From the diary of
Louisa May Alcott

October 8, 1879

Dear Marmee's birthday. Never forgotten. Lovely day. Go to Sleepy Hollow with flowers. Her grave is green, black berry vines with red leaves trail over it. A little white stone with her initials is at the head, & among the tall grass over her breast a little bird had made a nest. Empty now, but a pretty symbol of the refuge that tender bosom always was for all feeble and sweet things. Her favorite asters bloomed all about, & the pines sang overhead.

I have no romantic feelings about age. Either you are interesting at any age or you are not. There is nothing particularly interesting about being old—or being young, for that matter.

—Katharine Hepburn

Try to keep your soul young and quivering right up to old age.

—George Sand

Great Birthday Gifts to Give and Receive

• A full or half day at your favorite spa. Be sure to have dinner reservations to continue the "relaxing" trend later that evening.

• A scrapbook of pictures and mementos (cards, napkins with a fun greeting, party favors) from your surprise birthday party.

• A trip back home:
Return to your birthplace or
hometown for a unique celebration. Visit the hospital where you
were born, play hopscotch on the
playground of the elementary
school you attended, and
so on.

• Breakfast in bed
followed by eighteen
holes of golf followed by
lunch at the country
club.

Portrait of a Birthday

Evelyn's friend, Mrs. Threadgoode, encourages Evelyn to take up a job selling Mary Kay cosmetics.

Evelyn Couch, how can you say that, you are still a young woman. Forty-eight years old is just a baby! You've got half your life left to live yet! Mary Kay doesn't care how old you are. She's no spring chicken herself.

—Fannie Flagg, *Fried Green Tomatoes at the Whistle Stop Cafe*

We are all the same people as we were at three, six, ten, or twenty years old. More noticeably so, perhaps, at six or seven, because we were not pretending so much then.

—Agatha Christie

Each age, like every individual, has its own characteristic intoxication.

—Will Durant

From *The Railway Children*
by Edith Nesbit

"That's a likely little brooch you've got on, Miss," said Perks the Porter; "I don't know as ever I see a thing more like a buttercup without it was a buttercup."

"Yes," said Bobbie, glad and flushed by this approval. "I always thought it was more like a buttercup almost than even a real one,—and I never thought it would come to be mine, my very own—and then Mother gave it to me for my birthday."

"Oh—have you had a birthday?" said Perks; and he seemed quite surprised, as though a birthday were a thing only granted to a favoured few.

"Yes," said Bobbie; "when's your birthday, Mr. Perks?" The children were taking tea with Mr. Perks in the Porter's room among the lamps and the railway almanacs. They had brought their own cups and some jam turnovers. Mr. Perks made tea in a beer can, as usual, and every one felt very happy and confidential.

"My birthday?" said Perks, tipping some more dark brown tea out of the can into Peter's cup. "I give up keeping of my birthday afore you was born."

"But you must have been born sometime, you know," said Phyllis, thoughtfully, "even if it was twenty years ago—or thirty or sixty or seventy."

"Not so long as that, Missie," Perks grinned as he answered. "If you really want to know, it was thirty-two years ago, come the fifteenth of this month."

"Then why don't you keep it?" asked Phyllis.

"I've got something else to keep besides birthdays," said Perks, briefly.

"Oh! What?" asked Phyllis, eagerly, "not secrets?"

"No," said Perks, "the kids and the Missus."

It was this talk that set the children thinking, and, presently, talking. Perks was, on the whole, the dearest friend they had made. Not so grand as the Station Master, but more approachable—less powerful than the old gentleman, but more confidential.

"It seems horrid that nobody keeps his birthday," said Bobbie. "Couldn't we do something?"

"Let's go up to the Canal bridge and talk it over," said Peter.

Whatever wrinkles I got, I enjoyed getting them.

—Ava Gardner

If you survive long enough,
you're revered—rather like an
old building.

—Katharine Hepburn

In early Egypt and Babylon, birthday parties were unheard of for the lower classes. Only kings, queens, and noblemen acknowledged the day they were born, let alone celebrated it.

Old age is always fifteen years older than I am.

—Bernard Baruch

Do not deprive me of my age.
I have earned it.

—May Sarton

The Most Wonderful Day of the Year 271

When I Was One-and-Twenty

When I was one-and-twenty
I heard a wise man say,
"Give crowns and pounds and guineas
But not your heart away;
Give pearls away and rubies
But keep your fancy free."
But I was one-and-twenty,
No use to talk to me.

When I was one-and-twenty
I heard him say again,
"The heart out of the bosom
Was never given in vain;
'Tis paid with sighs a plenty
And sold for endless rue."
And I am two-and-twenty,
And oh, 'tis true, 'tis true.

—A. E. Housman

The spiritual eyesight improves as the physical eyesight declines.

—Plato

The Most Wonderful Day of the Year 275

To become young again, no.
To become younger than I ever
was, yes!

—Colette

Ripeness is all.

—William Shakespeare

Portrait of a Birthday

A group of friends known as the "Mamas" celebrate their friend Willa's birthday with characteristic joie de vivre.

We did one three-day stint of painting the weekend of Willa's fifty-third birthday. Creedence Clearwater was the music of the day, and there was food and wine. In the late afternoon, the Mamas jumped buck naked off the floating dock that extended into the river, and we swam and splashed. . . .

—Colette Dowling, *Red Hot Mamas*

Very early, I knew that the only object in life was to grow.

—Margaret Fuller

May you live to be a hundred years
With one extra year to repent.

—Traditional Irish toast

[The birthday is] a big event in everybody's life. It should be a holiday—with pay.

—Michael Darling

Fun Things to Do on Your Birthday

• Indulge in a day of beauty (facial, manicure, and pedicure), either at a salon or in the comfort of your own home.

• Throw a backyard "beach party" or other theme-style party such as a luau or circus/carnival party. Decorate, serve food, and dress to fit the theme.

• Have
a good old-fashioned
slumber party (no matter
what your age). Rent
favorite movies, make some
popcorn, gossip, and behave
as if you were sixteen
again.

• Make
each and every
meal a celebration by
eating breakfast, lunch,
and dinner at three
favorite restaurants.

A man hath no better thing under the sun, than to eat, and to drink, and to be merry.

—Ecclesiastes 8:15

I have never admitted that I am
more than twenty-nine, or thirty at
the most.

—Oscar Wilde

Rise and Shine

During the Middle Ages in Germany, peasants celebrated a child's birthday with a Kinderfeste (child is *Kind* in German). Kinderfestes began at dawn, when the child was awakened to a cake with burning candles. The candles were kept lit throughout the day and replaced as they melted, until after dinner, when the cake was served as dessert. The number of candles on the cake

totaled one more than the child's actual age—the extra

candle representing the "light of life." The child, who

chose her favorite dish for dinner, also received presents.

Another Kinderfeste tradition that is no longer observed

was the anticipation of the Birthday Man. Children

hoped for a secret "visit" (much like a visit from Santa

Claus) from a bearded elf who would bring them extra

birthday gifts if they had behaved well all year.

Just to be is a blessing. Just to live
is holy.

—Rabbi Abraham Heschel

These years are still the years of my prime. It is important to recognize the years of one's prime; always remember that. . . . One's prime is elusive.

—Muriel Spark

I grow more intense as I age.

—Florida Scott-Maxwell

From *Little Lord Fauntleroy*
by Frances Hodgson Burnett

What a grand day it was when little Lord Fauntleroy's birthday arrived, and how his young lordship enjoyed it! How beautiful the park looked, filled with the thronging people dressed in their gayest and best, and with the flags flying from the tents and the top of the Castle! Nobody had staid away who could possibly come, because everybody was really glad that little Lord Fauntleroy was to be little Lord Fauntleroy still, and some day was to be the master of everything. Every one wanted to have a look at him. . . .

What scores and scores of people there were under the trees, and in the tents, and on the lawns! Farmers and farmers' wives in their Sunday suits and bonnets and shawls; girls and their sweethearts; children frolicking and chasing about; and old dames in red cloaks gossiping together.

. . . the sun shone and the flags fluttered and the games were played and the dances danced, and as the gayeties went on and the joyous afternoon passed, his little lordship was simply radiantly happy.

The whole world seemed beautiful to him.

Sweet things and pretty things ✸✸ all for your Birthday ✸

How Old Are You?

Age is a quality of mind.
If you have left your dreams behind,
If hope is cold,
If you no longer look ahead,
If your ambitions' fires are dead—
Then you are old.
But if from life you take the best,
If in life you keep the jest,
If love you hold;
No matter how the years go by,
No matter how the birthdays fly—
You are not old.

—H. S. Fritsch

The Most Wonderful Day of the Year 305

A

Birthday Blessing

Children wear brand-new clothes for their birthdays in India. After rising early in the morning, the family visits a shrine where the child is blessed. Later, the family might have a birthday meal of spicy stew and dessert consisting of rice pudding mixed with pistachios, raisins, and spices for dessert.

One changes from day to day . . . every few years one becomes a new being.

—George Sand

I've always felt proud of my age. I think people should be proud that they've been around long enough to have learned something.

—Frances Moore Lappé

From *The Song of the Lark*
by Willa Cather

One Saturday, late in June, Thea arrived early for her lesson. As she perched herself upon the piano stool,—a wobbly, old-fashioned thing that worked on a creaky screw,—she gave Wunsch a side glance, smiling. "You must not be cross to me to-day. This is my birthday."

"So?" he pointed to the keyboard.

After the lesson they went out to join Mrs. Kohler, who . . . came up with her trowel and told Thea it was lucky to have your birthday when the lindens were in bloom, and that she must go and look at the sweet peas. Wunsch accompanied her, and as they walked between the flower-beds he took Thea's hand.

"*Es flüstern und sprechen die Blumen,*"—he muttered. "You know that von Heine? *Im leuchtenden sommermorgen?*" He looked down at Thea and softly pressed her hand.

"No, I don't know it. What does *flüstern* mean?"

"*Flüstern?*—to whisper. You must begin now to know such things. That is necessary. How many birthdays?"

"Thirteen. I'm in my 'teens now. But how can I know words like that? I only know what you say at my lessons. They don't teach German at school. How can I learn?" . . .

Wunsch made a grimace, took his pupil's hand and drew her toward the grape arbor. "Hereafter I will more speak to you in German. Now, sit down and I will teach you for your birthday that little song. Ask me the words you do not know already. Now: *Im leuchtenden sommermorgen . . .*"

. . . I finally figured out the only reason to be alive is to enjoy it.

—Rita Mae Brown

From "To Princess Augusta of Homburg, November 28th, 1799"

Still kindly lingering the year from your eye departs,
And in hesperian mildness now faintly gleams
The winter sky above your gardens,
Evergreen arbours, poetic orchards.

And as I pondered here on your birthday, thought
What, thankful, I might offer, there still remained
Late flowers beside the pathway, fit to
Make you a crown that's alive, Augusta.

—Friedrich Hölderlin

The Most Wonderful Day of the Year 317

At twenty years of age the will reigns; at thirty the wit; at forty the judgment.

—Benjamin Franklin

Age has extremely little to do with anything that matters. The difference between one age and another is, as a rule, enormously exaggerated.

—Rose Macaulay

I'm Thirty-nine!

Certain birthdays seem to have more meaning than others—sweet sixteen (and never been kissed) and decade markers (turning thirty or the big five-O) are milestone birthdays for most Americans.

In certain cultures, however, some birthdays are

considered fortuitous and others are considered unlucky. The Chinese usually do not celebrate the fortieth and forty-first birthdays since the numbers sound like the Chinese word for "death." On the other hand, the Vietnamese consider forty, fifty, sixty, and seventy to be special numbers.

There was a star danced, and
under that I was born.

—William Shakespeare

Pleas'd to look forward, pleas'd to
   look behind,
And count each birthday with a
   grateful mind.

—Alexander Pope

If wrinkles must be written upon our brows, let them not be written upon the heart. The spirit should not grow old.

—James A. Garfield

In the midst of winter, I finally
learned that there was in me an
invincible summer.

—Albert Camus

Green Jade Cup

I don't complain that time passes too soon,
My only regret:
I've wasted my youth.
My gaze stretches afar toward a floating gossamer—
    a thread of my love;
A broken bridge and flowing river,
Sunset and drifting catkins—
Is that the spring's journey home?

—Kung Tzu-chen

The Most Wonderful Day of the Year 333

It is lovely, when I forget all birthdays, including my own, to find that somebody remembers me.

—Ellen Glasgow

Forget me not.

Most of us can remember a time when a birthday—especially if it was one's own—brightened the world as if a second sun had risen.

—Robert Lynd

From *The Picture of Dorian Gray*
by Oscar Wilde

"The soul is a terrible reality. It can be bought, and sold, and bartered away. It can be poisoned, or made perfect. There is a soul in each one of us. I know it."

"Do you feel quite sure of that, Dorian?"

"Quite sure."

"Ah! then it must be an illusion. The things one feels absolutely certain about are never true. That is the fatality of Faith, and the lesson of Romance. How grave you are! Don't be so serious. What have you or I to do with the superstitions of our age? No: we have given up our belief in the soul. Play me something. Play me a nocturne, Dorian, and, as you play, tell me, in a low voice, how you have kept your youth. You must have some secret. I am only ten years older than you are, and I am wrinkled, and worn, and yellow. You are really wonderful, Dorian. You have never looked more charming than you do tonight. You remind me of the day I saw you first. You were rather cheeky, very shy, and absolutely extraordinary. You have changed, of course, but not in appearance. I wish you would tell me your secret. To get back my youth I would do anything in the world, except take exercise, get up early, or be respectable. Youth! There is nothing like it. . . ."

I love my past. I love my present. I'm not ashamed of what I've had, and I'm not sad because I have it no longer.

—Colette

The secret of staying young is to live honestly, eat slowly, and lie about your age.

—Lucille Ball

The Passionate Pilgrim, No. 12

Crabbèd age and youth cannot live together:
Youth is full of pleasance, age is full of care;
Youth like summer morn, age like winter weather;
Youth like summer brave, age like winter bare.
Youth is full of sport, age's breath is short.
Youth is nimble, age is lame,
Youth is hot and bold, age is weak and cold.
Youth is wild and age is tame.
Age, I do abhor thee; youth, I do adore thee.
O my love, my love is young.
Age, I do defy thee. O sweet shepherd, hie thee,
For methinks thou stay'st too long.

—William Shakespeare

Let us never know what old age is.
Let us know the happiness time
brings, not count the years.

—Ausonius

May all your future years be free
From disappointment, care, or
   strife
That every birthday you will be
A little more in love with life.

—Anonymous

Grow old along with me!
The best is yet to be . . .

—Robert Browning

Book design and composition by Diane Hobbing of
Snap-Haus Graphics in Dumont, NJ

For Mr. Hood